KISS A MULE,
CURE A COLD
Omens, signs and sayings

Evelyn Jones Childers

ILLUSTRATED BY TIM LEE

Peachtree Publishers, Ltd.

Published by
PEACHTREE PUBLISHERS, LTD.
494 Armour Circle, N. E.
Atlanta, Georgia 30324

Manufactured in the United States of America

Illustrations and Cover Design by Tim Lee

Sixth printing (1995)

Library of Congress Catalog Card Number 88-60005

ISBN 0-934601-44-5

DEAR READER,

Folklore. When I was growing up we broke this word down into omens, sayings and signs. In fact I don't remember hearing the word *folklore*. But I did hear lots of omens, sayings and signs. We really needed to hear them, too. Sometimes I don't know what we'd have done without them. We counted on them to let us know what was going to happen in just a few minutes. Or the next day. Or even farther into the future.

Now I'll have to admit they let us down a lot of times. But when a letdown came, we didn't let it bother us. We just took it for a sign that something else was going to happen. It usually did, too.

Over the years my children, three sons, often heard me speak of omens, sayings and signs. As they grew older, they wanted me to write them down for them. So I've written the ones I remember, plus new ones I've heard from other people. I've also thrown in a few facts, myths and some other things I like. Enjoy.

Evelyn Jones Childers

CONTENTS

LOVE, MARRIAGE AND BABIES

Count the white spots on your middle fingernails on both hands to see how many boyfriends or girlfriends you have.

When you hear a turtledove calling, it's a sign somebody loves you and has sent the bird to tell you so.

Eating chocolate puts you in the mood for love. Other foods that should help your love life are apples, bananas, olives, tomatoes, catnip and ginseng. Eating chocolate can also help you get over a love affair. Keep plenty of tissues handy in case it also puts you in the mood for love.

If you allow someone to sweep under your feet, you won't get married within the year.

Sit on a table, marry when you are able.

During a marriage ceremony, stand with your feet going the same way as the cracks in the floor to ensure happiness.

If a woman walks under a ladder, she will not get married during the coming year.

Pull a chicken wishbone with someone else to see who will get married first. It will be the one who gets the shorter piece. To find out quickly who you will marry, put this piece of wishbone over an outside door. Then the next eligible person who comes through the door will be your future mate.

To dream of a death usually means you or someone you know will be getting married soon.

Marriages made in May are supposed to have lots of good fortune and happiness in them.

If a bride wears blue when she gets married, it means she will always be true. Red means she'll soon wish herself dead. Wear grey when you marry, and you'll live far away from the place you live at the time of the wedding. Wear brown and you'll live in town after

If a girl's breath steams up a mirror, she is no longer a virgin.

the ceremony. Marry in black and you'll soon wish yourself single again; yellow, you'll soon be wishing you had another fellow; green, you'll soon be ashamed to be seen. Wearing white shows you're marrying the right man for you. The bride who wears tan will soon be seen running around the town. Your spirits will soon sink if you wear pink. A bride in checks means she and her groom are star-crossed lovers. A bride in stripes may soon have stripes on her back. If you wear several colors to your wedding, confusion may soon reign in your marriage.

If the sun shines on a bride, she'll have a happy marriage. The bride who gets rained on will shed lots of tears in her marriage.

A bride who cries at her own wedding will have a very happy marriage.

A woman should take the first step she takes after getting married with her right foot.

If the hair from another woman's head in sewn into a bride's wedding dress, the bride's husband will be unfaithful to her.

If a bride will use a quilt having the turkey track design on her marriage bed, her husband will remain faithful.

If you marry a person whose name starts with the same initial as yours, it will not be a happy marriage.

When you mail your sweetheart a letter, place the postage stamp on upside down. This will show your love.

A "fast" woman can't make good applesauce.

The first time you travel a new road, if you'll stop and pick up a rock and put it in your pocket, the next person of the opposite sex that you shake hands with will be your future mate.

More people prefer to make love on Sunday than any other day of the week.

Do you ever when talking or just thinking unexpectedly say someone's name aloud? If so, it is supposed to be a sign that this person is thinking or talking about you.

Peel an apple, keeping the peeling in one long spiral. Gently twirl the peeling three times around your head, then drop it on the floor. It is supposed to form the first initial of your sweetheart's name as it lands. You can also toss the peeling over your left shoulder instead of twirling it around your head.

5

Dig the seeds out of an apple you've eaten. As you take each seed out say, while thinking of your sweetheart: "One I love, Two I love, Three I love I say. Four I love with all my heart, and five I cast away. Six I love, seven he loves, and eight we both love. Nine he comes, ten he tarries, eleven he courts, and twelve he marries." The number of seeds in the apple will also tell you how many children you and your sweetheart will have after you are married.

The love vine, a golden, slender vine, a parasite which lives sprawled across other plants, can be used to find out if your sweetheart loves you. Pull some of the vine away from the parent vine, and toss it onto some other plants. Name this new hunk of vine for your sweetheart. If it lives, then your sweetheart loves you.

Sprinkle some cornmeal around a table leg; then place a snail in the cornmeal. As the snail crawls around, it is supposed to spell out the name of your future mate.

Eat a thimble full of salt without drinking any water or speaking to anyone before you go to bed, and you'll dream of your future mate.

Write three names on three small slips of paper. On a fouth piece write the word *Unknown*. Fold all four into small wads. Next pack a coating of bread around each wad. Drop all four into a glass of water.

If you'll sleep with a piece of someone else's wedding cake under your pillow, you'll dream of your future mate.

You will marry the person whose name floats to the top first. If the paper with *Unknown* rises first, it means you have not yet met the one you will marry.

Light a kerosene lamp; set a glass of water in front of it, even with the flame. Look through the water at the flame. You should be able to see the face of the person you will marry. Another version of this is to place a glass of water in front of red coals in a fireplace and look through the glass to see whom you will marry in the coals. This one could be too rough and hot on the eyes.

Light a kerosene lamp, sit with your back to it, and look at the lamp flame in a mirror. In the mirror you are supposed to be able to see the one you will marry.

Here's another way to discover whom you'll marry. Cook a backward supper for two by preparing the entire meal with your hands behind your back. Never look to see what you are doing. Then, with the meal cooked and on the table and two places set, sit down at one of the place settings. Soon the one you are to marry is supposed to come in and sit down at the other place. If you are never to marry, a coffin will come rolling through the door and up to the table.

On the first day of May, carry a mirror to a dug well. Stand with your back to the open well, holding the mirror so that it reflects down on the water in the well. By looking at the water's surface in the mirror, you should be able to see the face of the one you are to marry.

Spend the last night of April at another's home. The next morning before any of the family are up, steal their dirty dishrag and start walking home with it. On the way you will meet the one you will someday marry. Once home, bury the dishrag.

Hunt a bird's nest in May. The number of eggs in the nest will be the number of years it will be before you get married. If you are already married, the number of eggs will be the number of children you will have.

During a new moon in May, look over your left shoulder at the moon, and say, "May moon, May moon, round and fair. Under my left foot I'll find a hair." Then look under your left foot. You are supposed to find a hair from the head of your future mate.

At any new moon, any month, look over your right shoulder and say, "New moon, new moon, do tell me who my own true love will be. The color of his hair, the color of his eyes and the day we will meet." That night you should dream the answers to what you asked.

9

If you can count nine stars for nine straight nights, on the ninth night you will dream of the one you will wed. You can do the same thing by winking twice at a star going to bed. You'll dream of your future mate.

When you stump your toe, if you'll kiss your thumb, you'll see your sweetheart before dark that day.

To patch up a lover's quarrel, set shoes you are wearing in the shape of a *T*, then say, "When my true love I long to see, I set my shoes in the shape of a *T*."

The first night you spend in a new home, name each of the four corners of the room you sleep in. The corner you look in first the next morning will bear the name of the one, out of the four, who likes you the best.

If you have cold hands, you have a warm heart.

At dusk go to a haunted house, taking a ball of twine. Once there, toss the twine out a window, but keep hold of the end of the string. This done, start rolling the twine back up, saying as you do, "Come my true love and wind my ball. Come my true love and wind my ball." Soon your true love should appear outside the window and start rolling up the ball of twine from that end.

The number of seeds in an apple will tell you how many children you and your sweetheart will have after you are married.

At a quilting bee, after a quilt has been stitched together and taken from the quilting frame, four single girls can tell who will get married first. They do this by each taking hold of a corner of the quilt. Next, someone else drops a cat into the center of the quilt. Whichever corner the cat comes off of, the girl holding that corner will be the next to get married. Of course, each girl hopes the cat will choose her corner. But I've seen the cat get so mad — squawking and screeching and scratching mad — as each girl tries to get it to choose her corner that pretty quick, even if a girl was planning on getting married the next week, she will gladly give up her chances just to keep the cat from choosing her corner to leave from.

To keep your lover, get a lock of his hair and put it with one of yours. Do this during a full moon. Now light a candle and burn both hairs at once in the flame while you say that as the moon grows smaller, so will your sweetie's desire to leave you.

To keep your lover: Take two fresh eggs and write your name on one and your sweetheart's on the other. Let both eggs stay in the refrigerator overnight, side by side. The next morning stir and cook both together in an omelet or pancakes. And be sure to eat both.

To keep your lover loving you forever try this: On the night of a new moon, tie pictures of you and your lover face to face with a red ribbon. Place them in the moonlight as you say that as the new moon grows larger, so may your lover's love for you grow stronger. Then put the two pictures in a safe place. If you think it is necessary, you can repeat this every new moon until you are completely sure of your lover.

Plant a house plant in a pot in your home. Place the plant in the light of the new moon and say that as the plant grows and blooms, so too will your lover's love and yours for him or her grow and become stronger.

Since red is the color of love and passion, burn two red candles under a new moon while saying that as the moon grows and gets bigger, your sweetheart's love for you will grow and get stronger.

To regain a lost love, burn salt three nights in a row by sprinkling some in a fireplace while you whisper your hope that your sweetie won't be able to rest until he or she comes back to you.

If you'll hide a turtledove's tongue somewhere on your body, it is supposed to bring you and your estranged lover back together.

To discover the profession of your future mate, go over all the buttons on your clothes, saying as you touch each button: "Rich man, poor man, beggarman, thief. Doctor, lawyer, Indian chief." The last button counted answers the question.

A love charm can be made by sewing an ounce of yarrow into a small square of flannel. Place this under your pillow at bedtime and say this: "Thou pretty herb of Venus's tree, thy true name is yarrow. Now who my bosom friend must be, pray tell thou me tomorrow." If this is properly done, it will reveal your future husband or wife in a vision just before you wake the following morning.

If a man sends his sweetheart yellow flowers, it means he is jealous of her.

If a pregnant woman carries her unborn child high, it will be a girl. If she carries low, the baby will be a boy.

If a woman who is expecting a baby walks under a ladder, she will carry the baby for eleven months instead of the usual nine.

If an expectant mother looks at a dead person, her baby will be very pale.

If a pregnant woman is frightened by something, say a snake, her baby will be born with a birthmark. To prevent the birthmark, she should grab the sides of her dress for a few seconds after the fright.

To help ease the pain of a baby's teething, string a dime with a hole bored in it, minted the year of the baby's birth, on a ribbon and tie it around the baby's neck. Or cut the feet off a mole and string them. Tie the string around the baby's neck to help with the teething problem. Another way to help a teething baby is to make a necklace of thread-salve balls. Let baby wear this necklace until its teeth are through.

Hill people used to believe that if a baby didn't fall off the bed before it was a year old, it wouldn't live to a ripe old age.

If a woman has a baby when she is aged forty, it means she will be capable of having children until she is fifty.

The deep wrinkles between a baby's knees and thighs will reveal what sex the next baby will be. One deep wrinkle per leg indicates it will be a girl. Two deep wrinkles mean it will be a boy.

If a baby talks before it walks, its tongue will be its ruin.

If you cut a baby's fingernails before it is a year old, it will steal when it is older.

A cat sitting near a sleeping baby's face will steal the baby's breath.

15

To cut the pain in childbirth, place an axe under the mother's bed. Another way to cut childbirth pain is to place scissors under the mother's mattress.

If you see a man and woman in front of the fireplace when you get up New Year's morning, you will be married before the year is out.

The first person you kiss after the new year begins will love you the most for the coming year.

To make magic pills that, when eaten at the stroke of midnight on Halloween, will reveal your lover to you in your dreams, use an ounce of butter, ten ounces of brown sugar, nine crushed hazelnuts, and one teaspoon of nutmeg. Mix thoroughly, and roll into nine pills. Eat.

On Halloween night, if a man crawls under a blackberry bush, he will see the shadow of his future wife.

A vision of her future husband will appear in the mirror of a girl who stands before the mirror combing her hair and eating an apple on Halloween night.

Weather

A ring around the moon is a sign there will soon be rain.

The number of stars inside the ring will indicate how many days will pass before rain, one star for each day.

If the moon is cupped up (lying on its back), it is holding water. This means rain can be expected in a very few days. If the moon is turned down, it's empty of water and no rain will fall for a few days.

A heavy dew in the morning foretells no rain for that day.

A dog eating grass means rain is due soon and that the dog is going to be sick.

Hanging a dead snake in a tree will cause rain soon. Turning a dead snake onto its back will, too.

In times of drought, all signs of rain fail. (Since this one is usually true, there's no point in fooling around with dead snakes during a drought.)

When maple trees show the undersides of their leaves, rain can be expected soon.

Birds and bats fly lower just before a storm.

Lightning bugs flying close to the ground signal rain will be here shortly. Lightning bugs flying as high as the treetops are a sign it will not rain before morning.

Smoke rising straight up from a chimney indicates a day of lovely weather ahead. Smoke from a chimney does the reverse before a storm. It comes down low toward the ground and messes about.

Bees return home to their hives when a storm is nearing.

Fish come to the surface just before a storm.

All insects are more active for about twelve hours before a storm is due, up until about two hours before the storm arrives. Then the insects become very inactive. Quiet. Still.

When bad weather is coming, especially snow, sleet or high winds, cattle in a pasture will turn their rumps in the direction from which it will come.

When raindrops are big and round, they hardly ever wet the ground. When raindrops are small, a lot of rain can be expected to fall. So much, in fact, the creek might rise.

Rainfall mixed with sunshine means the devil is whipping his wife. It also means this is only a partial shower — part of it today and then part of it tomorrow at the same time. (These showers are also very beautiful.)

Red sails (clouds) at night, sailors' delight. Red sails at morning, sailors take warning.

Signs of rain to come: dampness in the saltcellar, corn blades curling in the sun, horses refusing to drink.

When storm clouds appear and you have yard-run turkeys, watch them. If they turn their backsides to the wind, letting their tail feathers stand on end, there's likely to be some hail in the coming storm.

When it is unusually quiet so that the sound of fowl, especially guineas, can be heard a long way, it means rain is in the making and will be here shortly.

If you have yard-run chickens, by watching them, you can tell when a rainy spell is near an end. The chickens will start pecking and preening their feathers.

Chickens going to roost early usually means a storm is due.

Hogs carrying sticks for a bed is a sign of bad weather coming.

Crickets chirping louder than usual is a storm warning.

When chickens roost high in trees, it means no rain for about a week.

An unusual number of flies, mosquitoes and snakes also indicates a storm to come. This is especially true if the flies cling to you as though they have molasses on their feet.

When you see a lot of pretty girls out walking, especially on a Sunday afternoon, it usually means it will rain soon, most likely the next day.

When a lot of jets leave trails across the sky, rain will be coming within the next day or two.

A rooster crowing after he is already on the roost means his head will be wet before morning.

22

When you see a rainbow after a shower, you'll know there is not supposed to be any more rain for a while. Clear weather coming up.

In certain parts of India it is thought that it will bring rain during times of drought if two frogs are put through a marriage ceremony.

When the wind starts blowing steadily from the east, falling weather — rain, sleet, snow — can be expected soon.

If you have a wet June, you will have a dry September; if you have a dry June, you will have a wet September.

If it rains on the first day of dog days, it will rain for the entire forty days of dog days. If it doesn't rain the first day of dog days, it won't rain for the next forty days. During dog days, dogs are supposed to be more apt to go mad. Other wild animals were, at least once, thought to be affected in the same way. During dog days, snakes are thought to be blind and very angry; therefore, they will strike at anything they hear. Also, mockingbirds don't sing during dog days.

When there is a greenish-yellow tint on storm clouds or just in the air, seek shelter. This color often indicates a developing tornado or one already developed. There will at least be a lot of wind and hail coming shortly.

To determine Fahrenheit temperature, count the number of chirps a cricket makes in fourteen seconds and add forty.

24

If it rains on July 15, it will rain for the next forty days.

If it rains on your Easter parade, it will rain for the next seven days or the next seven Sundays.

You can expect at least one big storm at about the time winter changes into spring.

A light snowfall after the first of the year that melts in a few hours is called a "robin snow."

Fog over a pond of water on an autumn or spring evening warns of a frost that night.

The first frost of the coming winter will be three months after you hear the first cicada of the summer.

If it thunders in December or in February, it will frost in May.

The call of the first whippoorwill in the spring signals the end of cold weather.

In the spring, if kingfishers build their nests in the creek banks down close to the water, it will be a dry summer. If it is to be a wet summer, they will construct their homes high above the water lest their nests be flooded during the coming summer.

To predict an upcoming winter, split a persimmon seed in half. Inside you should find the outline of an eating utensil — a spoon, fork or knife. A spoon means it will be a mild winter; a fork, a medium to mild winter; a knife, a rough to very severe winter.

The best time of year for meteor showers is August.

In the summertime, if you hear no insect sounds, the temperature is either over 105 degrees or under forty.

If the hornets build their nests close to the ground, it will be a very bad winter with lots of snow on the ground. If hornets build their nests high, it will be a mild winter.

After eating all the meat off a chicken breast bone, hold it toward a light. If you can see through it, the next day should be a pretty day.

When oak wood crackles, pops and shoots off sparks while burning, it is said to be popping up a snow.

A flock of crows flying about while cawing and crowing means there is a huge wind coming shortly.

When the family cat turns its backside to the fireplace, winter and colder weather are at the door.

Rabbits playing in a dusty road is a dry weather sign.

In autumn, when all the flies outdoors are trying to come indoors, it indicates that cold weather will be here in just a day or two.

When there are a lot of blackberry blooms in spring, it means the coming winter will be a cold, bad one.

If the summer onions have thin skins, a mild winter is coming up.

There will be one snow in the coming winter for every fog in August.

One sign of an approaching bad winter is that "Woolly-the-Worm" will have a thick, very dark coat of fuzz. If the winter is to be mild, he will have a light-colored coat of fuzz. Woolly-the-Worm's body can also be divided into three segments to foretell the weather for fall, winter and early spring. The darker the portions, the more cold, snow and wind there will be. The darker Woolly's center, between the two dark ends, is, the colder, more severe the winter will be.

There will be a larger than usual persimmon crop and a heavy nut crop in the fall before a bad winter.

When ants crawl in single file, rain is on the way.

Just before winter starts, if the moon's path is north of the path of the sun in early evening, the winter will be cold. If the moon's route is south of the sun's, it will be a warmer winter.

Thunder just before or during a snowstorm means you can expect several inches of snow to accumulate.

If a snow lies on the ground for three days, more snow will fall on it.

Snow that crosses itself while falling indicates that the storm will be heavy.

After you eat all the meat off the Thanksgiving turkey, examine its breast bone. The darker the bone, the colder the winter coming up.

The sound of frogs croaking beside streams indicates that spring is nearly here. So does an abundance of earthworms near the surface of the ground.

In spring, if you hear a whippoorwill first on one hill and then on another, it means lots of warm sunshine is coming up. It also means it is time to plant cotton.

Frogs and tree toads croak more just before a storm.

Legend had it that December 25 through January 5 are the "ruling days" for the weather in the upcoming year. The weather on Christmas Day will be the predominant weather in January; February's weather will be like that of December 26; and so on.

Grasshoppers sing only when the temperature is above eighty-four degrees.

If all the food placed on a table at a meal is eaten, then the next day will have pretty weather.

When a healed broken bone starts to ache, it's a sign that there is bad weather coming soon.

When you find a lot of dead limbs off nearby trees on the ground early of a morning, you can expect rain shortly.

Birds will fly high when fair weather is coming and low if bad weather is approaching.

Gardening & Household Chores

When planting corn, plant four kernels to the hill: one for the blackbird, one for the crow, one for the cutworm, and one to grow.

Corn should be planted on the increase of the moon so the waxing moon will burst the kernel. In three moons' time, the corn will have reached its tallest leaf.

Corn should be planted in the spring of the year when oak leaves are the size of a squirrel's ear.

Corn planted on a decreasing moon will have a big stalk and little ears, but corn planted on an increasing moon will have little stalks and nice big ears. The dark of the moon is when the moon is decreasing; the light, when it is increasing. A new moon is at its smallest and starting to grow. An old moon is at its largest and starting to decrease.

To keep crows from taking up young corn plants, place a string or rope around the corn rows.

Oats need to be planted in the light of the moon, or you won't make enough to feed a coon.

Cutting when the moon is new in August completely kills Johnson grass, roots and all.

Sweet potatoes should be harvested on the decrease of the moon so they can cure without rotting. In fact, the last five days of the decrease, the last quarter, of the moon is best. The last quarter of the moon is when the right side of the moon looks like someone has mashed it in.

Sweet potatoes should be stored or banked in dirt for curing or placed in lots of pine straw.

The best time to plant root crops — beets, potatoes, etc. — is when the signs are in the feet. Or at least below the knees. Potatoes will make even better if this can be done on the dark of the moon. Above ground crops — beans, tomatoes, etc. — should be planted when the signs are in the arms. But I've found about any crop produces well when the signs are in the feet — or at least below the knees.

If you plant green snap beans when the signs are in the bowels, the beans will bloom themselves to death, but there will be very few beans.

Plant green (snap) beans on Good Friday, and they are supposed to make, come hell or high water.

Don't plant anything in your garden on "rotten" Saturday. If you do, the seeds will rot in the ground . . . definitely not grow. Good Friday is the Friday before Easter Sunday, the day Christ died on the cross. Rotten Saturday is the day Christ lay in the tomb.

If you cut or trim your hair several times on the first quarter of the moon, it will gradually become bulkier and have more body.

When you kill a hog on the dark of the moon, little grease or fat will cook out of the meat. If you butcher a hog on the light of the moon, so much grease will come out of it as it cooks, you will begin to wonder if the meat is all grease. The lard rendered from a hog butchered on the light of the moon will turn rancid in a very short time. Soap made from such lard will turn clothes yellow if used in washing.

If house shingles are laid on the increase of the moon, they will curl and the roof will leak. If the shingles are laid on a decreasing moon, they will lie flat and the roof will not leak.

If a split-rail fence is laid on the decrease of the moon, the bottom rail will sink into the ground.

In summer, when the sap is in the trees, cut wood on the full of the moon. This will drive the sap out, and the wood will cure white instead of being stained by the sap.

Pulpwood cut in April and May on the dark of the moon can be peeled easily. You can even use a straightened-out hoe to peel the bark off. In September you can peel pulpwood cut on the full of the moon easily with an axe. But if it is cut on the wrong time of the moon, the bark sticks tighter than the skin on a hide-bound bull.

Plant seed potatoes with the eyes turned up so the potatoes will come up sooner.

Don't plant onions and potatoes on the same side of the garden.

To prevent Irish potatoes from sprouting, put an apple or two in with them.

37

Harvest your onion crop after the tops fall over during the week just before a full moon. Let the tops stay on until they are dry. Store onions in a dry place.

One way to dry onions is to tie them up, each separated by a knot, in old panty hose. Hang in a dry place.

One way to prevent home-grown potatoes from rotting as they cure is to sprinkle lime on the place where you'll place the potatoes. Then, after placing the potatoes, sprinkle more lime over them. To keep home-grown potatoes from turning green as they cure, protect them from light. You can do this by placing newspapers with some holes punched in them over the potatoes. Also, when placing the potatoes for curing, make only one layer and leave a space between potatoes.

After the potatoes are cured and then pull a fast one on you along about December by sprouting, stop them from ruining (at least for a while) by gently, with your hands, brushing off the sprouts.

To keep cutworms from cutting down your tomato plants, stick a nail or a stick about the size of a pencil down beside the stem of each plant. Or place a paper collar around each tomato stem, above and reaching slightly below ground level.

For tomatoes to grow and produce better, dirt should cover not only the roots but also the stem up to the first limb of the plant.

To make tomatoes grow by leaps and bounds, dissolve a birth control pill in about a pint of water and pour the mixture around the roots of the plant every week or so.

If someone gives you a plant, don't thank the person for it and the plant will live and grow better.

A tomato plant will stop growing taller if you pinch off the tip of the main stem when the plant has reached the height you wish it to be.

To grow an extra large tomato, watermelon, pumpkin, etc., remove all but a couple of each fruit or vegetable from the vine.

To raise twin pumpkins or watermelons, etc., glue two seeds together and plant them when the signs are in the twins.

To prevent large cabbage heads from splitting as they grow, get a firm grip on the head and give it a one-fourth turn. This will break a few of the roots and the plant will take in less water, thereby not growing so fast that it bursts.

To keep your seeds from clumping together during planting, sprinkle and rub some talcum powder over and through them.

To protect your strawberries from birds, wrap black electrical tape around a six-foot length of old hose, thus making a "fake snake." Place this in your strawberry bed.

To get rid of poison ivy, spray the area with a solution of soapy water mixed with three pounds of salt per two gallons. A few sprayings of this mixture should kill the poison ivy.

Plant a border of marigolds around your garden to help keep out nibblers — rodents, groundhogs, raccoons, etc. Or spray a solution of one tablespoon liquid hot sauce per gallon of water on your vegetable plants as they first come up. Repeat every so often, especially after a rain.

To help keep the birds from eating the seeds out of your sunflowers, especially the seeds you want to save for next year's planting, tie a "bonnet" of cheesecloth loosely over the flowers when they are mature.

To kill unwanted weeds growing in your driveway or any place, pour boiling salted water over them.

To keep moles out of your garden, place a couple of windmills in it. The vibrations from the windmills will repel moles.

To keep grass from growing between bricks or stones in a walkway, sprinkle the spaces with salt every so often.

Sprinkle salt around wells, springs, water pipes, etc., to help prevent snails from crawling into the water supply and contaminating it.

Chives are believed by many to repel aphids from roses, so plant some among your rose bushes. This also works for lettuce and peas. An added bonus will be that you can use the chives in salads and other dishes.

Garlic planted in a garden mixed in with the other plants is believed by many people to repel insects.

Some people believe yarrow and tansy will repel insects such as Japanese beetles, ants and flies; therefore, they plant it in and around their gardens.

If you plant marigolds in your garden to help repel insects and rodents, don't plant it near pepper plants or the pepper will taste like the marigolds.

To help keep groundhogs from eating out of your garden, throw some smelly sneakers about. The sneakers will also repel crows by working on the same principle as a scarecrow — the human scent drives the birds away.

Mothballs tossed about in your garden are supposed to help keep rodents and insects out, but the fresh air tends to deplete the mothball odor. Placing mothballs in bean hills with the bean seeds does help keep moles from eating the seeds.

Garlic is supposed to deter, repel or discourage Japanese beetles, aphids, mice and moles. Planted around peach trees, garlic will discourage peach borers, and planted near green (snap) beans, it has the same effect on bean bugs. When planted near rosebushes, garlic is supposed to help them develop resistance to black spot and mildew.

Basil planted in pots or in the ground repels mosquitoes and flies. Therefore, it is a good plant near any outdoor sitting area.

Snap beans planted near Irish potatoes help keep Mexican bean beetles and potato bugs away.

Flour sprinkled between rows of vegetables will coat cabbage worms as they crawl through it, thereby killing the worms. Flour will also coat and kill any slugs that crawl through it.

Beer left in pans between garden rows will draw slugs. Then the slugs will fall into the beer and drown.

Lettuce leaves left out at night between garden rows are supposed to lure slugs under them. The next morning you can collect the slugs and dispose of them.

Marigolds planted close to snap beans, roses or any other plant, are supposed to deter Japanese beetles. Planted in with Irish potatoes, they help keep the potato bugs away.

Mints, especially spearmint, planted near buildings are supposed to help keep ants away. Mints planted in a garden are helpful in keeping cabbage worms from laying their eggs among the vegetables.

Daffodil bulbs planted near tulip and azaleas will help ward off such pests as moles, mice, chipmunks and other rodents.

Soybeans planted near corn help keep chinch bugs and Japanese beetles away.

Onion skins placed in cucumber hills are supposed to deter squash bugs from getting at the cucumbers.

Green black walnut fronds placed in a building or near an open sitting area will keep fleas away. When the walnut leaves dry out, they need to be replaced.

Sliced cucumbers placed where roaches like to run will cause the roaches to leave.

Cloves scattered around where ants like to play will cause the ants to hunt another playground.

To rid your home of fleas try placing a shallow pan of soapy water with a small light shining directly on the water. Leave out overnight. The fleas should jump at the light and fall into the water. Or try tossing a few flea collars around the house behind furniture or in other places children won't find them.

Deter ants by washing counter tops, floors and cabinets with equal parts of vinegar and water.

Hill people once believed that plowing land in January would ruin it for the next seven years.

The best time to transplant young fruit trees is in March. Actually, March is the best time to transplant any growing plant.

Plants, trees, etc., should be pruned when the leaves are off; March is usually best.

Lots of fall acorns mean a bumper fruit crop the next year. Dark nights in February are also a sign of a good fruit crop to come, as is thunder in February.

To make pecan trees start to produce, try driving a lot of rusty nails into the trunks.

To make watermelons taste their best, place them on blocks of wood when they are growing so that they receive the most sun possible.

To find out if a watermelon lying in the field is ripe, cut a small hole in it and pull out the plug to check the color. Another way to find out if a field watermelon is ripe is to place a broom straw across it. If the straw just lies there unmoving, the melon is still green. If the straw moves from crosswise to lengthwise, the melon is ripe.

You can kill a tree by girthing it, that is, by cutting off all the bark all the way around the tree for a width of a least twelve inches. I once saw a pine tree girthed by a heavy metal chain left lying around the entire trunk. The tree died.

A hole dug during a full moon has less dirt in it than a hole dug at other times. If you want to refill the hole later, you won't have enough dirt.

47

To hold vines or limbs of rose bushes, etc., while rooting them, pin them to the ground with plastic hairpins.

To keep your bushes blooming with a lot of roses, as each one dies, cut off the hip left on the bush.

Sow your winter turnips on July 25, and you'll make a good crop no matter if the weather is then rainy or dry.

Cut the sprouts out of your garden or any place you want to get rid of them on the ninth day of May, and they will die completely, roots and all.

When gathering winter squash, leave an inch or two of stem, and the squash will store longer. Or smear the stem end with soft wax, and the squash will store longer. An old melted-down candle stub can be used for the wax.

Only the female, never the male, holly tree produces berries.

To help deter ants, sprinkle some whole cloves, mint leaves or white vinegar along their routes.

HOME REMEDIES

Do not use any of these without first asking your doctor!

Vinegar-soaked brown paper placed on a sprain will ease pain and help with healing.

Drinking buttermilk liberally laced with black pepper helps get measle bumps out on a patient and then keep them out. Sheep pill tea is supposed to have the same effect.

A gob of spider webs and soot placed over a cut is supposed to stop the bleeding.

Ice placed on the nape of the neck will stop a nosebleed. A sliced onion placed there is also supposed to stop a nosebleed. Or try placing something metal, such as a case knife, flat against the base of the skull of someone with a noseblced. Another nosebleed treatment is to fold a small piece of brown paper and stick it under the person's upper lip.

Drinking black pepper tea can start a late period.

Having someone with chicken pox sit under a chicken roost may bring about a quick cure. If the patient can't sit under the roost, try scaring the chickens off the roost so that they will fly over the patient.

A faint bottle, made of whiskey and camphor, is good to have on hand to wave under the nose of someone who faints.

An asafetida bag worn around your neck will ward off all diseases, as should a necklace of garlic on a string.

Peeled onions hung in a room where sickness is will help kill the germs. They will also prevent visitors to the room from catching the illness.

A liver-growed baby can be cured by turning the child head over heels, completely, three times. Another cure is to measure the child seven times with a string and then burn the string.

A black string tied around a child's neck is supposed to cure or even prevent croup.

Sassafras tea soothes a stomachache. It also thins your blood in the spring.

If you eat three messes of poke sallet in the spring, you won't have typhoid fever that year. (But be careful how you cook the poke sallet or you won't be around long enough to have anything.)

A tea made by boiling pine needles in water has lots of vitamin C, thus making good emergency nourishment if you are lost in the wilderness.

As soon as possible after chiggers attach themselves to you, cover them with a coat of colorless nail polish. This will smother them to death and keep you from itching badly.

Apply witch hazel to mosquito or flea bites to relieve the itching.

Moistened antacid tablets rubbed on insect stings or bites help ease the pain. Spraying the bites with an antiperspirant will also relieve pain and itching.

To prevent bugs from biting you in the first place, spray any exposed skin with an antiperspirant before going outside in very buggy areas.

For a bee sting, try applying wet salt to draw out the venom. Or use moistened tobacco, wet baking soda or wet aspirin. Moistened meat tenderizer also works very well.

Squirting flying insects with hair spray will keep them away from you.

Soak four ounces of dried willow bark, per quart of water, for six hours. Bring to a boil and simmer for ten minutes. Strain. Rub on itching skin. This concoction will also help to make crow's feet disappear from around your eyes when applied there.

Daily use of a hair dryer is believed by many to prevent nits and lice from getting a toehold on a person's head.

For a snake bite, you can try grabbing up a live chicken, splitting it open, and placing the hot flesh over the bite. This should draw out the poison. A bottle of turpentine turned up over the bite has the same effect. A wad of chewed tobacco placed on a snake bite will draw out the poison. So will burning the snake in a fire.

Chewing birch or willow bark will relieve a headache.

Spraying yourself and your clothes with deodorant before a hike in the woods should keep you from getting poison oak. If you do become infected, spraying deodorant on the inflamed areas will relieve pain.

To ease the pain of an earache, catch a bessie bug from under an old log. Break the head off the bug, and put the drop of blood you find into the infected ear. Another treatment for earache is to heat the heart of an onion and place it in the patient's ear. Then wrap the head in a wool scarf to hold in the heat. Or heat a wool or flannel scarf and hold it next to the aching ear. Heating a drop or two of sweet oil and placing it in the ear along with some cotton should also work.

If you have internal worms, you are supposed to get rid of them by wearing your dress or shirt backward. You can also get rid of the worms by chewing some tobacco and swallowing the juice.

If you have a tapeworm, try to get rid of it by holding a cup of sugar in front of your open mouth. When the tapeworm comes up to taste the sugar, grab hold of its head and pull it out.

Another cure for internal worms is to eat a spoonful of sugar on which a drop or two of turpentine has been dribbled. The sugar is supposed to attract the worms; then the turpentine finishes them off. Or boil some horehound in water until it makes a syrup. Then take a spoonful or two. Another worm treatment is made with some Jersualem oakweed mixed with some cough syrup and formed into balls. Take one of the balls when needed.

For a ringworm, smear some of the juice from a black walnut hull on it. Repeat every so often until the ringworm is gone. Or wet three of your fingers, one at a time, and run each over the ringworm saying: "Ringworm, go away. Ringworm, go away."

To get over a hangover quickly, when you can stand solid food, eat it. And keep on eating as much as you can. Liquids are fine, but solid food will sober a person up a lot quicker.

For a migraine headache, soak a towel in vinegar and wrap it around your head.

For "just a headache," drink a half cup of tea with a shot of whiskey and honey in it. Then go to bed.

For a headache, sprinkle some brown paper with vinegar and place the paper on your head. Lie down in a dark room. Or try lying down and placing a fresh lemon peel across your forehead.

A poultice made from mandrake and periwinkle is supposed to cure skin cancers. This same poultice is also supposed to take off warts and, when placed over blood poisoning, to heal it.

Picking up a rock and spitting under it can get rid of warts. Or tie as many small rocks as you have warts in a rag and bury it. When the rag rots, the warts should be gone. Another remedy for warts is to steal a dishrag and hide it in a stump.

Rub your warts with kernels of corn, bore a hole in a tree, and stuff the corn in the hole. Then plug it up. Rub the wart with raw meat, then feed the meat to a dog. Or rub the wart with corn and feed the corn to a rooster. Dandelion juice rubbed on warts should also get rid of them. Rub the wart with a cut Irish potato, then bury the potato at the stroke of midnight. Or steal a dishrag and apply castor oil to the wart twice a day.

Try sucking a lemon or sipping some ginger ale to settle your stomach.

Treat nausea by placing a copper penny on your navel.

Some people find drinking a raw egg dropped into a glass of milk and cream helps to settle their stomach. Chewing birch bark can help also.

Catnip tea is good for easing the pain of colic, and it helps relieve gas.

Peach tree bark scraped off the tree with a downward motion and made into a tea helps to stop vomiting. Scraped off with an upward motion, the bark, made into a tea, cures loose bowels.

A cup of hot, strong lemonade helps ease stomach cramps.

Another treatment for an upset stomach is to squeeze the juice from one lemon into a drinking glass, add seltzer water and drink quickly.

Peppermint tea is a great help in relieving gas and aiding digestion. Sipping wine also aids digestion.

For ulcers, try two tablespoons of olive oil with or followed by six ounces of sweet milk.

For constipation, try mixing equal amounts of aloe plant and honey, and take a teaspoon as needed. Also try fig and olive oils.

Some foods that will help to control diarrhea are bananas, applesauce, rice, cinnamon and toast.

To help prevent diarrhea, especially when traveling, make a mixture of one-half teaspoon each of baking soda and salt. Add four tablespoons of sugar and one liter of carbonated water. Sip all through the day.

Barley gruel is good for dysentery because it will coat the intestines. If you add one or two drops of turpentine, it will help ease intestinal pain.

Boiled milk will help to bind up loose bowels. A thin mixture of flour and water will, also. Papaya tea is also good for diarrhea.

When drinking tea or a gruel, always sip it. Small sips.

Blackberry wine is a great help for the summer complaint: intestinal problems that include vomiting, nausea and dysentery. A tea of blackberry roots will also be a big help with summer complaint.

For acne, dab some toothpaste on the blemishes and let it dry. Another way to get rid of acne is to wash your face in a diaper wet by a baby. You can also place a mixture of grated cucumber and vaseline on the face.

If you'll wash your face in the first frost in fall, you will have a lovely white complexion.

To cure a hangover headache, eat some raw cabbage dipped in vinegar.

Smear some buttermilk on your face and let it dry overnight. When you wash it off, you should have a white complexion free of any freckles or other blemishes you might have had.

To rid yourself of dandruff, rub some warm peanut oil into your scalp. top with lemon juice and shampoo. Three or four applications, and the dandruff should be gone for good.

Leave some oak chips in water for several hours. Strain. This solution, when applied to the skin for several minutes daily is supposed to lighten freckles.

The following will ease the pain of a sting: a paste made of soda and buttermilk, mud, a wad of chewed tobacco, pastes of wet snuff or a strong laundry soap, such as Octagon, a slice of raw onion, a paste made from moistened activated charcoal, an ice cube, the juice of an aloe plant.

Aloe juice, when gently patted on shingles, will help take the sting, itch and hurt out of them.

The juices of the aloe plant, jewelweed and the plantain help when they are rubbed on areas infected by poison oak. Gunpowder mixed with sweet corn and rubbed on the infected area also seems to help.

Heat rash or prickly heat, can be greatly relieved by sprinkling talcum powder over it.

A fresh papaya leaf dampened and placed over skin ulcers, boils or swellings helps them to heal.

If you do have a cut or sore and get dew in it, especially during dog days, it will make the sore worse and cause it to take a long time to heal.

Swelling and bruises will heal faster if you place fresh lemon peels over them. Or soak some mullein leaves in vinegar and place them over the swellings and bruises to speed their recovery.

For an abcess, soak some white bread or biscuits in milk. Drain. Place the soaked bread on the abcess.

To prevent a cut from becoming infected, place a green grape leaf on it.

For a sore mouth, slosh some yellow root tea around in the mouth.

For an infected cut, beat some banana peels into a pulp and place on the infection. Or make a poultice of dampened white granulated sugar and place on it.

To stop hiccups, place your hands over your ears and swallow three times.

A poultice made from foxglove will help or cure gangrene.

For felons, scrape some bark off a seven-bark tree. Mix this will some meal or flour and dampen. Place on the felon.

For just any old kind of sore, mix together some sheep tallow and turpentine and place the mixture on the sore. Or place a mixture of lard and sulphur on the sore.

For athlete's foot, what farmers use to call police foot, use some hot cow or horse manure.

Hiccup Cures:

a. Fill a glass with tap water, then bend over until you can drink from the side of the glass farthest away from your body. Drink the entire glass of water.
b. Place some ice cubes in the space between your collar bones and neck.
c. Try sucking on ice.
d. Try drinking as much cold carbonated drink as you can at one gulp.
e. Drink a glass of water with a case knife stuck down in the water.
f. Place a tablespoon of peanut butter on the roof of your mouth. Slowly eat it, and when you finish the hiccups should be gone.

g. Try making the person with hiccups mad or scare the person.
h. Hold your hands firmly over your ears, palms toward ears. Do this for about ten minutes. Repeat the next day if necessary.
i. Eat a tablespoon of salt.

I found the following cures in an old health book I have:
a. Hold your breath as long as possible.
b. Swallow cold water.
c. Gargle while holding your breath.
d. Cough.
e. Sneeze.
f. Swallow a small piece of ice.
g. Swallow a sip of vinegar.
h. Put a pinch of salt on the back of your tongue.
i. Breath into a paper bag.
j. Apply an ice pack to the back of the neck.
k. Put a small amount of pressure on your ribs near the place the diaphragm connects.

Relieve eye strain by placing two damp lemon peels over your closed eyelids. Lie down and relax.

For inflamed eyes, make a helpful water by squeezing some fresh strawberries. Strain and let settle. Soak a cloth in the mixture and place it over the eyes. Leave the cloth there for about twenty minutes.

To get rid of a stye, rub a gold ring over the eyelid.

Eating sunflower seeds is supposed to strengthen your eyes.

To help get rid of bags under your eyes, especially early of a morning, place wet tea bags over your "bags." Or use sliced cucumbers.

Some things which should help you get to sleep if taken just at bedtime are warm milk, hot lemonade, orangeade, cold grapefruit juice or a tea made from chamomile, catnip or hops.

To help you remember your dreams, tape a paper clip or just stick a band-aid across your forehead just before you go to bed. As you put the reminder on your head, tell yourself that you'll wake when you have a dream and write it down.

To help to bring a boil to a head, tie a piece of fat meat over it or put the skipping out of an eggshell over it. You can also use poultices made of flaxseed, oatmeal, castor oil and white sugar, or a scraped raw Irish potato.

To help deter nausea when you have a fever, try sipping a mixture of Jell-O and water.

A great help for chills and fever is a tea made from wild cherry and dogwood barks. Chop the barks up into small pieces. Boil them in water for at least ten minutes; then let the tea steep for a few more minutes. Sip. A variation on this tea adds wahoo bark to the mixture.

For fever and ague, take one teaspoon of salt mixed in water. Then put a spoonful of salt inside each stocking or sock as soon as you feel a chill coming on.

For headaches and low fevers, soak one ounce of willow bark per quart of water for six hours. Bring to a boil. Simmer ten minutes. Strain. Drink. But don't drink more than three cups a day.

To help you to feel better when you have the flu, try drinking hot tea with a spoonful of raspberry jam added to it. Red raspberry tea also relieves nausea.

For a fever, chew some willow bark.

For a minor fever, lie down and place a damp lemon peel under each armpit.

If you will go barefooted in the summertime enough so that the bottoms of your feet get tough, you won't have many colds or sore throats the following winter.

For a cold, munch a clove of garlic, then drink a cup or two of peppermint tea.

For a sore throat, sip some slippery elm bark tea.

For a cough due to a cold, put a quarter teaspoon of ginger in a cup of hot water. Sweeten with honey and drink.

You can ease a sore throat by chopping up a raw onion, putting it in an old sock and tying the sock around your neck. Another old sock treatment is to warm some salt and put it in the sock and wear it around your neck. Or just tie an old dirty sock by itself around your neck and wear it.

For a sore throat, as an added help when you gargle warm salty water, try to sing as you gargle.

To help a sore throat or maybe keep it away all together, gargle some lemon juice.

To cure a sore throat, put kerosene on a dirty, worn sock and tie it around your neck. Also gargle salt water.

A tea made from Life-Everlasting (rabbit tobacco) is supposed to be good for a cold. It will also cure constipation.

For laryngitis, put some honey in your mouth and let it lie against the back of your throat for a few minutes. Then let the honey slowly seep down your throat. Another treatment for laryngitis is to gargle with vinegar, rain water and salt several times a day. For laryngitis or a cold, try gargling and slowly drinking a mixture of lemon or lime juice, honey and rum several times a day.

For a cold, drink a cup of regular tea to which you have added a tablespoon each of honey and whiskey and a teaspoon each of butter and cinnamon. Drink this as hot as you can stand it. Then go to bed and rest.

It is supposed to help get rid of a cold if you'll gargle with tabasco sauce, ten drops, in a cup of warm water. Another cure for a cold is to place some chopped onions or garlic under your pillow.

A good cough syrup can be made by dissolving some rock candy in a bottle of whiskey. Sip as needed. Another cough syrup can be made by boiling some pine buds for about fifteen minutes. Take out the buds and sweeten the water and residue with honey or sugar. Red-oak bark taken from the north side of the tree, boiled in water, and then sweetened with honey also makes a good cough syrup. Another one can be made by boiling the leaves, flowers and roots of the mullein plant. Let the mixture boil for about fifteen minutes. Strain. Sip when needed.

Ginger tea with some lemon juice added is a great help for colds. Drink the tea. Go to bed and sweat the cold out. Ginger tea to which some whiskey has been added will also help to cure a cold. With it, too, you drink the tea, go to bed and sweat the cold out of your system.

For a chest cold, make a poultice of onions (chopped and fried in grease), lard and cornmeal. Put this mixture on a flannel cloth, warm and then place on the patient's chest.

To loosen the congestion from a chest cold, fry some onions in grease, then smear the concoction on the patient's chest.

You can try to keep the colds away altogether by smearing your entire body in bear grease. If you don't want grease smeared all over you, you should be able to keep colds away by catching an oak leaf before it touches the ground. Or you can hang pieces of peeled onions over each of your doorways from October until the following May.

You can cure a cold by kissing a mule.

For croup, chest colds, etc., place a heated cloth poultice of pine tar on the patient's chest. The poultice is made like this: Use a piece of wool or flannel cloth about fourteen inches square. On half of this cloth smear a layer of pine tar, black sticky stuff that can be bought at a drugstore. On top of the pine tar, smear a layer of lard. Next, smear on a layer of camphor salve. Fold the rest of the cloth over all this mixture. Heat the entire thing, but don't let it get too hot. Place on the patient's chest. If you'd like to make your own pine tar, you can do it this way: Chop up some rich pine splinters. Dig a hole in a clay bank. Place a flat rock in the hole. On the rock place the pine splinters and set them afire. Be sure you have positioned the flat rock so that the pine tar, as it cooks out of the splinters, will run off the rock and into a container. Also be sure to put a cover of some kind over the splinters so that as they are burning, the pine tar will boil out instead of burning up. If you use any of this pine tar for medicinal purposes, dilute it with grease, as it is very strong and might blister a person.

To prevent rheumatism, steal an Irish potato and carry it in your pocket. You can also carry buckshot, a horse chestnut, or a buckeye. A copper bracelet or a copper wire worn as a bracelet will ward off rheumatism, as will sleeping with your work shoes under the head of your bed.

Rubbing lemon juice on inflamed arthritic joints will help to lessen the pain. Or soak some mullein leaves in vinegar and wrap them over the arthritic joints to help ease the pain. Cucumber bark beat into a pulp and placed on the arthritis pain will help. So will drinking tea made from cucumber bark.

For piles, or hemorrhoids, steep some pine needles in hot water and then hold your piles over the steam.

To make a salve to use on piles, boil some wall-ink in water until it boils down to a syrupy mess. Wall-ink is a plant that grows alongside branches or near ponds and swampy places.

The juice from the heart plant, when rubbed on piles, is supposed to cure them.

Sleeping on damp bedclothes will bring on pneumonia.

Burning chicken feathers in a fireplace in the patient's room is supposed to be a cure for pneumonia.

A person born with a caul can cure the thrush (or thrash). A child born after the death of its father can also cure the thrush, as can the seventh son of a seventh son. A man who has never seen his father is supposed to be able to cure the thrush by blowing three times in the patient's mouth. He can also cure rickets and hives the same way.

To cure asthma in a child, cut a green sycamore stick the height of the child. Then place the stick in a dry place, such as an attic, and let it dry out. When the child has grown taller than the stick, the asthma should be cured. Or measure the child with a string. Store it in a safe place. Once again, when the child has grown taller than the string, the asthma should be gone. Or take an old hornet's nest, pour boiling water over it. Steep. Drink the tea.

For a toothache, wet a small cloth with brandy. Place the cloth on the bad tooth.

Oil of cloves is another toothache remedy.

Spirits of nitre mixed with alum, put on cotton and placed on the tooth, will also ease the toothache pain.

If a toothache pain goes up toward the eye, take some horseradish leaves, remove the stems, wet and apply to the face over the pain.

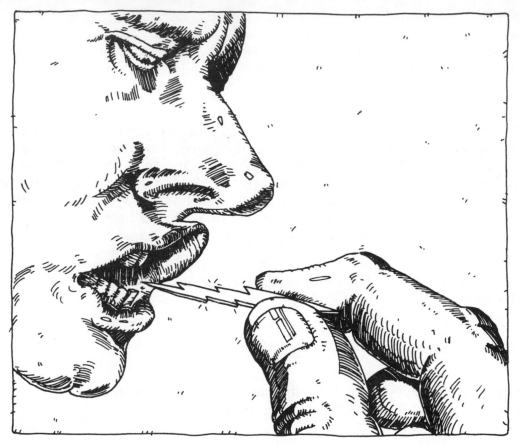

A splinter from a lightning-struck tree that is used as a toothpick will ease the pain of a toothache.

Place some ice on the skin between your thumb and index finger on the same side of your body as a toothache. Leave for about ten minutes to relieve pain.

For a country-style toothbrush, break off a small limb or twig from a black-gum bush. Make the brush about six inches long, peel off bark for about an inch, then gently chew until this inch is soft and pliable. Use it by dipping the soft end in a mixture of salt and soda held in the palm of one hand and then polishing your teeth.

To help make your mouth taste and smell better, gently brush your tongue with lemon juice.

Gargling with lemon juice greatly helps bad breath.

If foot odor is a problem, lemon juice rubbed over the feet should stop it temporarily.

To aid the circulation in your feet, give yourself a ginger foot bath for about fifteen minutes. Or soak your feet in hot water to which you have added two tablespoons of baking soda, or Epsom salts.

For leg cramps, pull off your shoes and turn them upside down. Not wearing any shoes? Turn a pair upside down under your bed.

To cure dropsy, make a tea using water and chestnut leaves. Make a lot and drink in place of water. Or use a pinch of bitter herbs, one of dried spruce bark, one of sarsaparilla, another of dried dye leaves, and a lump of salt peter the size of a bantam hen egg. Boil all together. Then put the mixture into a gallon of whiskey and add some rock candy. Drink three grams a day.

Grandma Jones used to chew foxglove for "a-hurtin' round her heart." Grandma was a smart woman since foxglove is the plant from which digitalis is made, and digitalis is one of the medications prescribed for certain heart problems.

A poultice made of vinegar and spider webs will help heal a nail puncture.

If a nail puncture becomes infected, smoke it over some smoldering wool rags in a metal bucket. Another way to smoke your nail puncture is to hold the wound over smoldering green pine needles.

To help draw the infection out of a nail wound, make a poultice of water mixed with cornmeal. Heat. Place over the wound in a clean cloth. Tie in place.

An onion or an apple a day keeps the doctor away.

A small rag filled with camphor pieces worn someplace on your body is supposed to help ward off germs, especially cold germs. Garlic and resin mixed together and worn someplace on your body will also keep away germs.

Place a burn in cold water or let cool tap water run over it.

Aloe juice, vaseline or white granulated sugar placed on a burn will ease pain and foster healing.

Some people claim they can talk the fire out of a burn by doing and saying this: Place hand on burn. Blow on it and say, "Old clod beneath the clay, burn away. In the name of God be healed."

To help you to feel better all over and relieve tension, place some fresh-cut roses in your room. Or home.

To help you to get to sleep, place some violets in your bedroom.

The color green helps to soothe nerves and promotes general healing.

Thirty drops of white vinegar in an ounce of water makes a good solution for cleaning your ears. Use a dropper to put in ear.

If your side hurts when walking, pick up a rock and spit under it to stop the pain.

When you have a thirst that nothing seems to help, drink a glass of cold buttermilk.

For a quick burst of energy, eat a spoonful or so of honey. Honey also helps to calm your nerves.

Blackberry wine will give you an appetite and settle your stomach. Homemade blackberry wine will also help to build up your blood.

Queen-of-the-Meadow root tea will keep your kidneys working correctly.

Horehound tea will help the pain of a sinus headache.

Pat a tea-soaked cloth on a sunburn to help ease the pain. Or wet a cloth in milk to which ice cubes and a couple tablespoons of salt have been added. Place on the sunburned area for about fifteen minutes. Do this several times a day.

One way to make dandelion tea is by boiling both the tops and flowers for ten minutes in water. Strain out the leaves. Add some honey to taste.

Farm Animals, Fowl, Insects & Other Creatures

Geese and ducks should be plucked when the moon is new because they will have more down than at any other time.

To prevent penned chickens from flying over a fence, pull a couple of feathers from only one wing of each fowl to upset their balance when they attempt to fly.

To stop a hen from being broody (wanting to hatch some baby chicks from eggs), dip the hen in cold water.

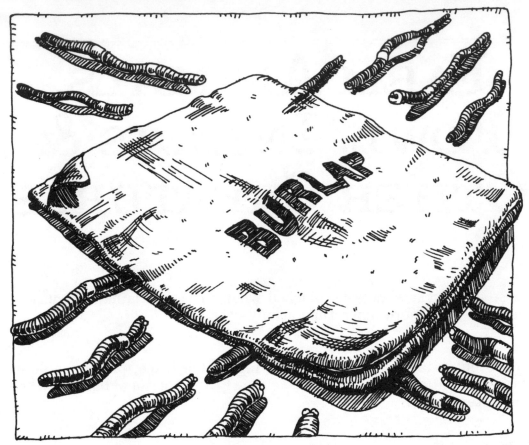

To attract earthworms for fishing, place a burlap sack on the ground. The worms will gather under the sack.

If you will carry the eggs you wish to place under a broody hen in a woman's bonnet or apron, the eggs are supposed to hatch out pullets (girl chickens). But if you carry the eggs in a man's hat, the new chicks are supposed to hatch out roosters.

Baby chicks should be hatched before May so they will grow to be better chickens.

A setting of eggs usually consists of twelve to fifteen eggs, about what the broody hen can comfortably cover with her body and wings.

Geese that wait until after March 17 to lay their eggs will have a bad year, and their baby goslings won't do as well as they should.

As far as the bull is concerned, a cow is bred when she is so tired she lies down.

If a cow has lost her cud, give her a greasy dishrag to chew on.

If a cow has the hollow tail, split the tail and put in a mixture of turpentine and lard. Another remedy for the hollow tail is to split the skin of the tail where it joins the cow's body and put plenty of salt and pepper in the slit. How can you tell if a cow has the hollow tail? One way is to note how she walks. If she has trouble making her hind legs work right, then it might be the hollow tail.

If the cow has trouble making her front legs work right, she could have the hollow horn. One remedy for the hollow horn is to bore a hole at the base of the horn, put in a mixture of salt and pepper, and plug the hole back up with a small wooden peg.

If a cow is string-halted, she'll walk with her back bowed up and have a problem making both her front and back legs work right as she walks. You can try to cure a string-halted cow by giving her a dose of salts (not salt) with a teaspoon of kerosene dribbled in it.

When a family buys a milk cow from a neighbor, the cow will do better and give more milk if the new owners name her for the lady of the house of her former owner.

When plowing up a field or garden with a mule (or horse), tell the mule to turn right by saying "Gee!" and to turn left by saying "Haw!" If you overhear someone giving out with a heartfelt "Oh, lordy!" you will know that the mule didn't know its "Gee" from its "Haw."

To prevent horses and other livestock from crossing a wooden plank bridge, take a couple of planks out of the bridge. Animals will be afraid to cross for fear one of their feet might go through the opening.

If you want mules or other animals to go someplace they don't want to, blindfold them first, then lead.

Pigs born when the signs are in the heart will be larger and healthier than pigs born when the signs are in the stomach. Stomach-sign pigs will be all belly.

When you wish to wean any farm animal, start when the signs are just below the knees. Then, as the signs move down and out through the feet, the baby animal will no longer want the breast.

A pig, calf, colt, etc., should be castrated when the signs are below the secrets so that the soreness will quickly be over with.

Castrate an animal, especially a pig, when the signs are in the heart, and you'll have a very hard time getting the bleeding to stop.

The meat from hogs that haven't been castrated before they are butchered will taste strong and gamy. It will also smell bad while being cooked.

Cut off a pig's tail and the pig will fatten out on a lot less feed than otherwise would be necessary.

Fresh pork can be cured by rubbing all pieces of meat thoroughly with salt, then placing the meat in a wooden box, preferably oak, into which about four inches of salt has been poured. With the meat in place, pour more salt over it until it is entirely covered.

If you raise turkeys, remember they are very curious critters. Therefore, when it rains, they will stare up toward the sky to see where the moisture is coming from . . . and will drown.

Martin gourds should always face west, or the martins won't use them.

If your dog has tangled with a skunk, to help get rid of the odor rub the dog in vinegar or tomato juice. You could also throw it in the creek. I don't think I could get close enough to a skunky dog to rub it with anything.

I've been told there are seven different kinds of meat in a turtle. I don't eat turtles myself. I've also been told these meats have the flavors of chicken, pork, beef, mutton, fish, goat and, of course, turtle.

I've also been told that if a turtle bites you, it won't turn loose until it thunders.

Holding a skunk's tail down over its scent glands won't prevent it from discharging its horrible odor.

I know this for a fact since it happened to one of my nephews: Even though a streaked field lizard doesn't have any teeth, one became desperate and closed its mouth so tightly on my nephew's arm that a mark, an outline of the lizard's mouth, was left behind.

To settle a swarm of bees, ring bells, beat on pans, do anything to make a lot of racket, and the bees will come down out of the air and cling to some earth-bound object.

Anything painted a pale blue is supposed to repel flies.

White or orange will repel mosquitoes, but dark blue, brown or dark red will attract them.

Yellow jackets are drawn to the aromas of perfume, soft drinks and meat.

Bees like the colors blue and yellow.

Smear some kerosene around your ankles and wrists when beginning a walk in the woods. This will help to repel chiggers.

You can tell a cow's age by counting the rings at the base of her horns.

Fireflies blink when they wish to attract a mate or another small flying insect for a meal.

A flea can leap one hundred times its own height and leap two hundred times the length of its body.

Only female, never male, mosquitoes bite humans.

When soldiers are marching in a straight line and disturb a rattlesnake, the third soldier will be bitten because the first soldier startles the snake, the snake coils as the second passes, and the third person is the one it strikes.

Not only can a cat bird imitate lots of other birds, but it can also sound exactly like a mewing cat.

If you live in a wooden house and have a problem with woodpeckers pecking holes in your home, tie some balloons shaped like snakes, owls, or other creatures which woodpeckers fear near the place they are ruining. Or try smearing a tequila cocktail on the house walls, when the birds peck into this mixture, it is supposed to burn their beaks. A tequila cocktail is made by mixing green turpentine and hot pepper sauce together with enough flour to hold the hot stuff together and allow it to stick on the walls.

A horse with four white feet and a white nose is an extra mean horse.

Brewer's yeast brushed on a dog's fur will get rid of any fleas the animal might have.

Wharf rats, thousand-legged worms and snakes and spiders can swim under water. Therefore, they can come up in your commodes, sinks, etc., and into your home.

When you kill a snake and leave it lying, its mate will come to it.

Poisonous snakes travel in pairs.

A horse hair left in water will eventually turn into a snake.

Soap will help to repel sharks, so before going swimming in the ocean rub it on your body and string a piece of soap around your neck.

Good Luck,
Bad Luck

If you see a penny lying on the ground, head side up, pick it up and you'll have good luck.

See a pin, pick it up, and you'll have good luck all day.

To have a cricket in your home is good luck.

For good luck, carry a buckeye on your person.

When moving into a new home, carry some salt first to ensure happiness and peace in the home. After you have the salt in, carry in a candle and some bread. The salt is so you will have the spice of life, the candle for light and warmth, the bread so that you'll always have food.

Nail a used horseshoe over the entrance to your home for good luck. Be sure the sides of the shoe are turned up to hold the good luck. If the horseshoe is nailed up with the sides turned down, all the good luck will run out.

According to the Legend of St. Joseph, if you are a Christian and want to sell your home, bury a statue of St. Joseph in your yard and the house will sell quickly.

When you think you need a little extra luck in something you've wished or hoped for, cross your fingers or kiss the first two fingers on your right hand or wet, in your mouth, the first finger on your right hand and hold it up for luck.

Wearing a red coral necklace is supposed to protect the wearer from storms and lightning. A red coral necklace placed under your pillow will protect you from nightmares, evil spirits and things that go bump in the night.

When looking for love, wear pink, the color of romance.

Carry a rabbit's foot, preferably the left hind one, for good luck.

If you wish on a new moon over your left shoulder, the wish is supposed to come true.

When you give someone a present of a wallet or pocketbook, put a coin in it for good luck and as a sign that the article will never be empty.

Make a wish on a red truck or car, and it is supposed to come true.

A person born with a caul is supposed to be able to foresee the future.

To help soothe your nerves, stay in a room painted a light green or a pale pink.

To attract a lover, burn a pink candle. This will also help you to feel better and bring you new friends.

If you want extra cash, try burning a green candle. Doing this is also supposed to help you to learn better and get your plants to grow better.

Growing a mustache strengthens a man's eyes.

If a large yellow good-news bee hovers about you, you are supposed to hear good news soon, most likely in a letter. A nice gesture on your part would be to tell the bee thank you. By the same token, if a bad-news bee, a small black bee, hovers about you, you will soon hear some bad news, probably in a letter. But you can counteract this by wetting your first finger, right hand, in your mouth, pointing at the bee and waving your finger about.

Make a wish and blow all the thistledown off a dandelion with one breath and the wish should come true.

A falling star means another soul has gone to Heaven. A wish made on a falling star is supposed to come true.

If you'll place a piece of silver outside on New Year's Eve, just before you go to bed, and then get up the next morning and bring the silver back indoors without first speaking to anyone else, you'll have plenty of money all the year long.

To be sure of good luck and having plenty to eat, eat black-eyed peas and hog jowls on New Year's Day. For the luck to work, every member of the family must have stirred the peas and jowls as they were cooking.

Early New Year's morning, gather a green bough and bring it indoors. Keep it inside your home for the entire year, and your income will be greater than your expenses.

If the first person to enter your home on New Year's Day is a man, preferably black-headed, you'll have good luck the coming year, especially with raising chickens.

It is a sign of very good luck to see cattle kneeling and hear them lowing at midnight on Christmas Eve.

Wearing at least three new items of clothing in your Easter outfit will bring good luck.

If your breakfast egg on Easter morning has two yolks in it, you'll have lots of money for the coming year.

It is good luck to have a wren live in your house or on the porch.

It is good luck to hear whippoorwills around your home. It is a sign of peace and good dreams.

For good luck throw a used horseshoe over your left shoulder.

To see a blue jay playing around your home is a sign you are soon going to have fun and good times. If you see a red cardinal around your home, it means you are soon going to receive some money.

If you kill the first snake you see in the spring, you're then supposed to be able to conquer your enemies for the rest of the year.

If you're trying to sell your house, paint it the color of sunshine . . . yellow . . . and it will sell quicker.

When first entering a house you are moving into, step first on your right foot, and you'll have good luck while living there.

A three-leaf clover stands for the Trinity. A four-leaf clover, the only thing Eve was allowed to bring out of the Garden of Eden, will bring you fame, success or a lover when you find one. Finding a five-leaf clover means you will soon receive some money, and a six-leaf clover means good health.

On New Year's Day if you take or throw anything out of your house without first bringing something into it, you'll have bad luck in the coming year.

It is bad luck for someone to spend New Year's Eve night but not the next night at your home. It is also bad luck for you to spend New Year's Eve night away from your home.

Washing clothes on New Year's Day might hasten the end of someone you know or wash away some friendships.

A broom placed on the doorsill will keep witches from entering your home even if the broom is hidden.

If you take the ashes out of the fireplace on New Year's Day, you will have bad luck.

Don't sweep the trash from your floors out the door on New Year's Day, or you'll be sweeping out your luck for the coming year.

It is good luck to bring holly into your home on Christmas Eve, but it is bad luck to bring it in before then.

If you kiss someone under the mistletoe at Christmas, the mistletoe should be burned before January 6 or the two of you will become enemies.

You should cut your Christmas cake before Christmas Eve to avoid bad luck.

If someone offers you an Easter egg, take it, or you will harm your friendship with the person offering you the egg.

It is bad luck to bring an axe or hoe indoors. If you must bring an axe or hoe indoors, remember to take it back out the same door you brought it in.

Stepping on a crack will break your mother's back.

A wild bird's getting into your home is a sign of bad luck. To counteract the luck, tie knots in a string.

Killing a toad will make the family milk cow go dry or the milk you have on hand go bad.

It is bad luck to open an umbrella indoors.

It is bad luck to step on a cloud reflected in a puddle.

If you see a penny on the ground tailside up, leave it alone, for if you pick it up you will have bad luck.

If a rocking chair rocks when no one is sitting in it, it is a sign of bad luck.

A black cat running across the road in front of you means bad luck. To counteract this luck if you are in a car or other vehicle, throw something out the window.

It is bad luck to sing in bed or before breakfast.

It is bad luck to walk under a ladder.

It is bad luck to walk with one shoe on and the other shoe off.

If you break a mirror, it could mean seven years of bad luck.

Spilling salt is supposed to attract bad luck. But it can be stopped by quickly grabbing the spilled salt and throwing it over your left shoulder.

When you start to leave your home and discover you have forgotten something and go back for it, be sure to sit down for a few seconds before leaving again — or you'll have bad luck while you are gone. If you're leaving on a trip and have to go back, counteract bad luck by walking out the door backwards the second time.

Watching a person leaving your home until they are out of sight will cause bad luck. But when you leave a place, look back at it and you will be sure to return there someday.

Placing your hat on a bed means bad luck.

Get up on the left side of the bed in the morning, and you'll have bad luck that day. Climbing over a footboard to get into bed is even worse bad luck.

It is bad luck to cut your toenails on Sunday.

Sneezing at the table is bad luck. So are counting stars and combing your hair after dark.

Planting a weeping willow tree means you will be doing a lot of weeping.

It is bad luck to plant a cedar tree, for when the tree is large enough to shade a grave, you'll likely be needing one.

Fruit trees that bloom twice in one year mean bad luck.

Burning old apple branches for firewood will bring bad luck.

It is bad luck to wash clothes before wearing them.

When you drop a book, be sure and step on it or you'll have bad luck.

It is bad luck to dream of cabbages or to propose to your sweetheart in church.

If a rooster crows at an unusual time, it means bad luck has already happened somewhere.

If two cabinet doors bump into each other when opened, it is bad luck.

If you accidentally put your underwear or socks on wrong side out, wear them this way or you'll have bad luck.

It is bad luck to move an old broom into a new house.

Sing while you are eating, and you'll cry before bedtime.

Don't eat at a table while wearing a hat or cap.

It is bad luck to burn lightning-struck wood.

Giving a person a present with a sharp edge, say a knife, scissors, etc., will cut your friendship in two.

It is bad luck for three people to light cigarettes off the same match or to burn sassafras wood in your home.

Don't sweep the trash off your floors out the door after dark.

It can be bad luck to cut out a garment on a Friday or to start making a garment on a Saturday and not be able to complete it that day. It is also bad luck to sew on Sunday. In fact, you just might have to pick out every stitch you sew with your nose.

It is bad luck to blow on a mirror and cloud it up, to put your shoes higher than your head, or to whistle in a cemetery.

Being the first one to leave a cemetery after a funeral is bad luck.

A whistling girl and a crowing hen always come to some bad end.

If you move into a new home on a Sunday, you'll soon be moving on to another house.

You should not look in a mirror in a house where a corpse is lying in state. If you do, bad luck is sure to come to you.

If you wear new clothes to a funeral, a member of the deceased's family will die within the same year.

If you play with or in fire, such as punching around in it with a poker a lot as it burns, you'll wet the bed that night.

When you visit in someone's home, leave by the same door you entered or you'll have bad luck.

Dreams, Omens, Myths & Facts

Dreams

If you eat three almonds just before bedtime, your dreams will be clear, sharp and in full color. You will remember them better, too.

If men eat pumpkin seeds at bedtime, they will have romantic dreams. If women want to have romantic dreams, they should eat blackstrap molasses at bedtime.

Doughnuts or any sweets at bedtime can cause you to have nightmares, especially about snakes. So can greasy foods.

Chocolate eaten at bedtime will cause lovely, romantic dreams.

To help you get to sleep, smear nutmeg oil on your forehead at bedtime or eat a tablespoon of honey.

If you dream of a snake, it is a sign you have an enemy.

If you dream of pigs, it means you will be asked for money.

The first time you sleep under a new quilt, whatever you dream is supposed to come true.

If you kill a snake in your dreams, it means you will conquer your real-life enemies when you are awake.

If you tell your dream before you eat breakfast, it is supposed to come true.

Omens

If your nose itches, it means someone is coming to see you. If it's the right side, a man is coming; the left side, a woman. If your entire nose itches, this indicates a lot of people are coming.

If a spider drops from a web in front of your face you will soon receive a letter.

If the palm of your right hand itches, you are soon going to shake hands with a stranger. If the palm of your left hand itches, you are going to receive some money.

When the bottom of your right foot itches, you are soon going to walk on strange ground. If the bottom of your left foot itches, it means you are soon going to kiss a fool.

When you are cooking a meal and drop the dishrag, it means someone is soon coming to your home.

Drop a knife, and it means a man is soon coming to see you. Drop a fork, and a woman is coming to your home. Drop a spoon, and a child will soon visit.

If you have bread and reach for more while eating, this is a sign someone more hungry than you is soon coming to your home.

If a rooster crows when it is standing in front of an outside door, it's a sign someone is soon coming to see you.

When your ear burns, it means someone somewhere is talking about you.

If your finger itches under your wedding ring, it means you have thoughts of straying on your mind.

If a lightning bug gets in your home at night, it means there will be one more or less in your home the next night.

Hold a buttercup under another person's chin. If it reflects a yellow spot there, then this person likes butter.

If you can kiss your own elbow, it will change your sex.

If you get wet in the first rain in May, getting wet in any other rain for the rest of the year won't make you sick.

You can go barefoot the first day of May and for the rest of the barefoot season without getting sick.

If you see fish jumping out of water, ants running from their hills, or other animals acting contrary to nature, a major natural disaster — earthquake, avalanche, rock slide — may be imminent.

Make a wish on a redbird, when you see one, and the wish is supposed to come true.

At the sound of the first whippoorwill in the spring, make a wish and roll over three times. If you prefer not to lie down on the ground and roll over, remain standing and turn three times repeating your wish each time you turn around. Your wish will come true.

To catch a wild bird easily, first sprinkle some salt on its tail.

When a candle is burning and you see a spark on the candle wick, it is supposed to be a sign that you will soon receive a letter. A long flame on a candle you've lit means cash is soon coming to you. To see a candle burning with a blue flame means there is a spirit present. Burn a gold candle to bring yourself more money.

If you see a butterfly first in the spring, you'll be pretty all the coming year. See a toad first and you'll be ugly all year long. See a lizard first and you'll be smart. See a snake first and you'll be lazy.

If the first butterfly you see in the spring is white, you'll hear of a death in the coming year. If the first is multi-colored, it means marriage for you or someone you know in the coming year. If you see a green butterfly first, it signals a divorce for you or someone you know in the coming year. A yellow butterfly seen first means you can expect a new baby in the family in the coming year. A black butterfly seen first means you can expect to take a trip during which you might have to face danger.

You can find out all that is going to happen to you in the coming year by going to a crossroads at daybreak on the first of May and listening to the wind.

Dropping a small piece of melted lead into cold water will help you to predict your future because the lead will take the shape of something to be closely associated with you in the future.

Bite the head off a butterfly, and you'll get a new outfit the color of that butterfly.

If your dress tail or jeans leg accidently turns up, kiss this place, and you'll soon get a new dress or pair of jeans.

A dog howling is supposed to foretell the death of someone. The direction the dog is looking as it howls indicates where this person lives.

The last person a dying person looks at will be the next person to die.

If a clock stops by itself in a house in which a body is lying in state, then another member of the family will die. Therefore, when someone dies, the family sometimes stops all the clocks by hand.

A screech owl screaming is a sign of approaching death for someone nearby.

When a body is lying in state, only the relatives of the deceased are supposed to use the back door until the body is buried.

When a member of a family dies and the family has bees, the bees must be told of the death by the oldest woman and the youngest relative of the deceased, or all the bees will leave.

In the days when a corpse wasn't embalmed, a vinegar-soaked cloth was placed over the face of the deceased to help preserve it. Silver coins were placed over the corpse's eyes to hold the lids closed. If no silver was available, nickels were used.

Some people think when you hear a mourning dove cooing, you will hear of a death shortly. Others think a mourning dove will cry and moan for a mountain man if he has no one else to cry for him when he dies.

In the Solomon Islands, people believe that your soul flies up to Heaven as a butterfly when you die.

At midnight on Halloween, go to a crossroads and listen to the wind. It is supposed to tell you all the things that are to happen to you in the coming year.

Whatever you do on New Year's Day — work, play, fight, etc., you will do things similar to these all through the new year.

A green Christmas, a warm sunshiny day, means a full cemetery during the coming year. A cold, blustery Christmas Day means an empty cemetery for the next year.

If you are out walking on Halloween night and hear footsteps behind you, don't look back — for it might be the dead following you.

Myths & Facts

Take any number up to ten. Double it. Add four. Divide by two. Take away the original number. The number left will be two.

Take any number greater than zero. Multiply it by three. Add one. Multiply by three. Add the original number. The answer will always end with three. Strike off the three and the number left will be the original number.

Take any three numbers in sequence, then reverse them and subtract the smaller from the larger. The result will always be 198. For example 123 would become 321. Subtract 123 from 321, and the answer is 198.

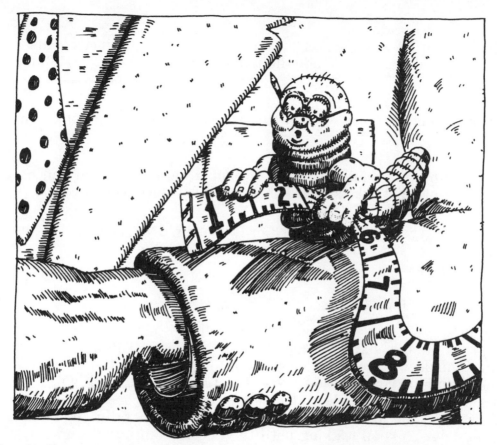

If an inchworm starts crawling on the clothes you are wearing, it means the worm is measuring you for a new outfit which should be coming soon.

115

Multiply nine by any number except zero and the product equals nine when reduced to a single digit. For example, $9 \times 2 = 18$ and $1 + 8 = 9$.

The first number, when spelled out, with an *A* in the spelling is a thousand.

Take a penny and double it every day for a month and you will have, at the end of thirty days, more than a million dollars.

There are fifty-six words in the Lord's Prayer, 118 words in Psalm 23, 271 in the Gettysburg Address, and 297 in the Ten Commandments.

How to dowse for water:

Some dowsers use a dogwood limb. This limb should be forked with two prongs about sixteen to eighteen inches long. The handle to the prongs should be about ten inches long. To use, hold the ends of the prongs, thumbs covering the ends. The trunk of the stick will dip down when over water. With hands and thumbs in place, start walking over the area in which you hope to locate water. When the end dips down, keep walking until the end is pointing straight down toward the ground. How deep underground the water is can be determined by counting the steps you make from the time the end of the stick starts dipping until it points straight down. The number of steps equals the number of feet to the water. Other dowsers may use limbs from other kinds of trees.

Always make sauerkraut when the signs are in the thighs or lower part of the legs and in the feet. If you make it at other times, the kraut will be slimy and no good. If you make homemade sauerkraut when the signs are in the secrets, the kraut will have such a bad odor while it's cooking you won't be able to stand it. Or eat it. Kraut will also have a very bad odor if a woman makes it when she is having her period.

There is an old wives' tale that when the devil left the Garden of Eden after his encounter with Adam and Eve onions sprang from his right hoofprint and garlic from his left. Maybe this story is what led to the belief that garlic will ward off vampires and other evil spirits.

If you pour bleach, such as Purex, into a tin measuring cup, the cup will become warm as far as the bleach reaches.

To help you have more energy, wear red; to help you calm down, wear or be around pink.

Oak and maple firewood burn about twice as long as pine or spruce.

A box painted black feels heavier than a white box of equal weight.

A pole, in surveying terms, is a distance of about sixteen and a half feet.

A cord of wood, cut and stacked, is four feet by four feet by eight feet. A face cord of wood, when cut and stacked, is four feet high, eight feet wide, and fireplace length.

Andirons are also called firedogs.

Brush arbors, where summer church revivals were often held in years past, were sometimes called lightning bug churches.

To remember how to spell geography, take the the first letter of each of the following words: George Ernest's oldest girl ran a pig home yesterday.

To spell Mississippi, remember this: *M - I* - crooked letter - crooked letter - *I* - crooked letter - crooked letter - *I* - humpback - humpback - *I*.

To find out a person's age and month of birth, ask the person to multiply his birth month by two. Then add five to this, and multiply

If birds use any hair from your head to build a nest, you will get a headache.

the answer by fifty. Next add his present age to this and subtract 365 from the results. Now ask the person for the number he has. To this you add 115. The numbers on the left in your answer will be the person's birth month; the numbers on the right will be his/her age.

Ways to make homemade dyes:
a. Onion skins boiled in water make a pale orange dye.
b. Orange peelings or golden rod stems and leaves or hickory bark make a yellow dye.
c. Sassafras roots make a pink dye.
d. Use red onion skins or fresh beet juice or red mud for a red dye.
e. Black walnut hulls make a dark brownish-yellow dye.

Except for the fresh beet juice, you should boil any of the above ingredients in water for several minutes. Strain if desired. Then place the material you wish to color in the hot water. Leave several minutes or until the material is the desired color. To set the dye, throw a handful or two of table salt into the water.

Place a wooden cross over your bed to keep ghosts out of your bedroom.

Lightning will not strike your house if you put a hunk from a lightning-struck tree under it.

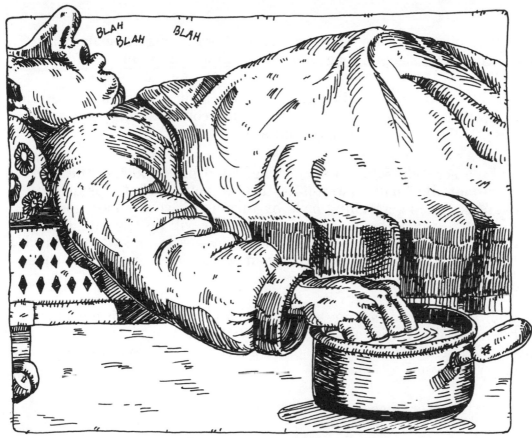

To get someone to talk in his sleep, place one of his hands in a pan of cold water.

When camping outdoors, to keep snakes from trying to share your bed, circle your sleeping bag or pallet with a hair rope.

If you bite your tongue while you are talking, it means you have told a lie or are fixing to. If a small, sore bump comes up on your tongue, it also means you have told a lie.

To make a screech owl stop screeching, lay a broom across the kitchen doorsill. Another way is to turn all your pockets inside out. You can also stop screeching owls by turning all your shoes upside down. Usually just the ones you are wearing will do the job. Pull them off and turn them upside down. If you are in bed when an owl starts screeching, get up and turn your work shoes or the last shoes you've worn upside down.

Custom dictates that anyone you greet on Christmas Eve morning with the words "Christmas Eve gift" must give you a gift before the day is over. However, if they use the greeting first, you must give them a gift.

Ghosts will never appear on Christmas Eve.

On January fifth, Old Christmas, bees will hum in their hives at midnight.